A DOZEN A DAY

BOOK

Pre-Practice
Technical Exercises
FOR THE PIANO

by

Edna-Mae Burnam

Exclusive Distributors:
Music Sales Limited, 14-15 Berners Street, London W1T 3LJ, UK.
Music Sales Pty Limited , 20 Resolution Drive, Caringbah, NSW 2229, Australia.

A DOZEN A DAY

Many people do physical exercises every morning before they go to work.

Likewise—we should give our fingers exercises every day BEFORE we begin our practising.

The purpose of this book is to help develop strong hands and flexible fingers.

Do not try to learn the entire first dozen exercises the first week you study this book! Just learn two or three exercises, and do them each day *before* practising. When these are mastered, add another, then another, and keep adding until the twelve can be played perfectly.

When the first dozen—Group I—have been mastered and perfected, Group II may be introduced in the same manner, and so on for the other Groups.

Many of these exercises may be transposed to different Keys. In fact, this should be encouraged.

EDNA-MAE BURNAM

CONTENTS

To Chris and Billy

Group I

1. Walking

2. Running

3. Skipping

4. Jumping

5. The Splits

6. Deep Breathing

7. Cartwheels

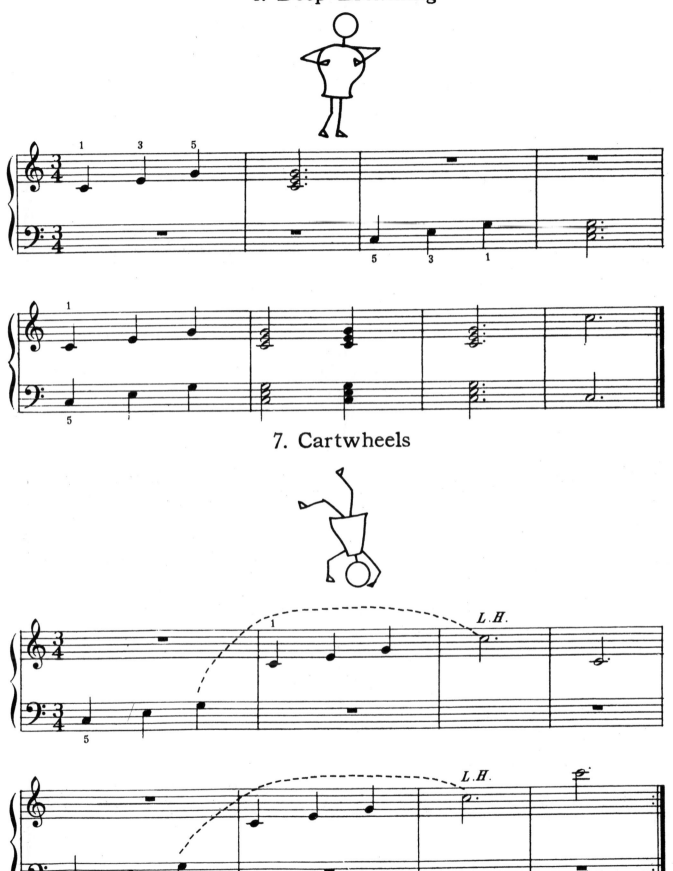

8. Deep Knee Bend

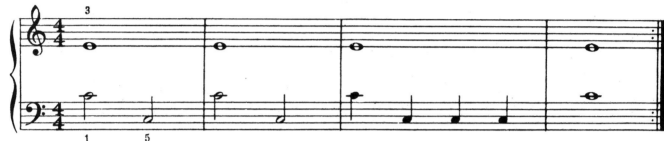

9. Hopping On Right Foot

10. Hopping On Left Foot

11. Standing On Head

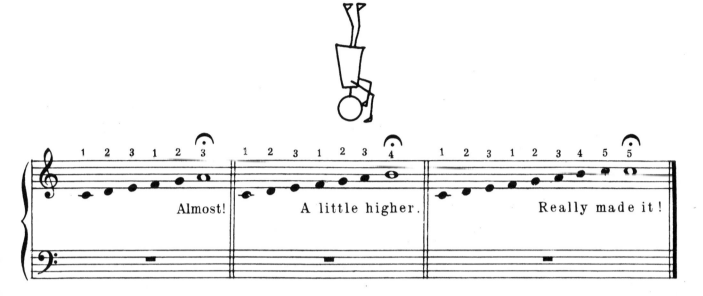

12. Fit As A Fiddle and Ready To Go

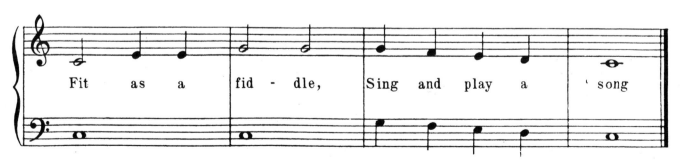

Group II

1. Stretching

2. Tiptoe Running

3. Jumping Off The Front Porch Steps

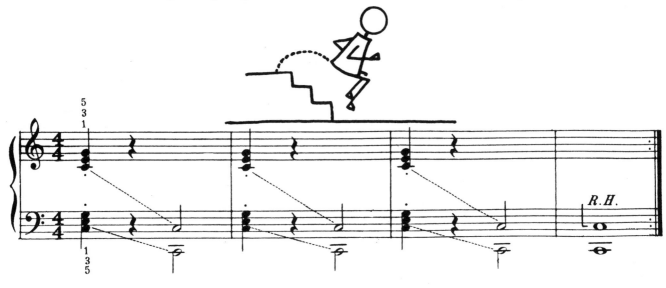

4. Climbing Up A Ladder

5. Going Down A Ladder

6. Jumping Like A Frog

7. Hanging From Bar by Right Hand

11. Swinging

12. Fit As A Fiddle and Ready To Go

Fit as a fid - dle, All day long;

Ex - er - cise will make my fin - gers ver - y strong.

Group III

1. Deep Breathing

2. Rolling

3. Cartwheels

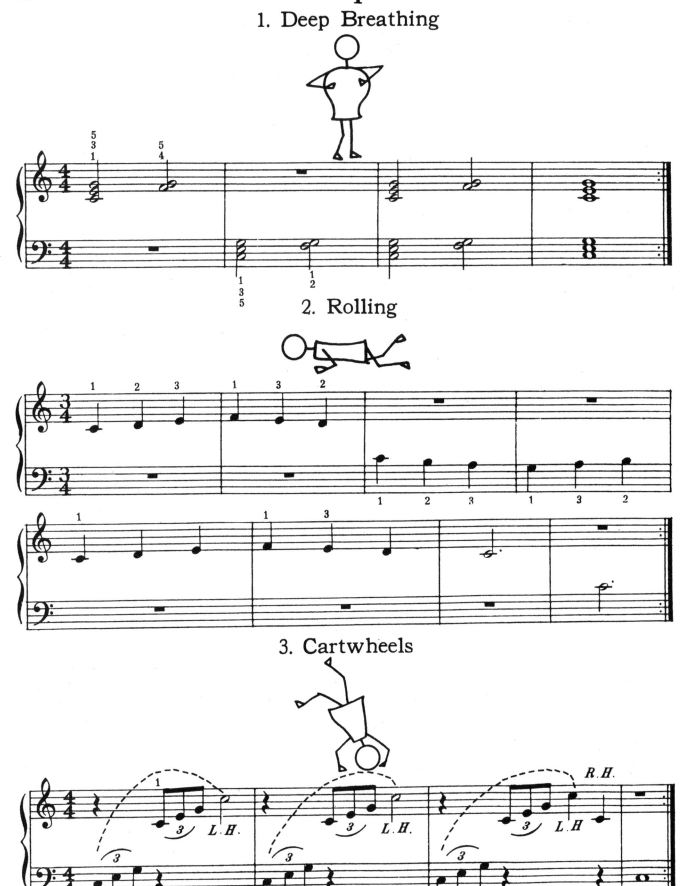

4. Skipping

5. Jumping Rope (Slow, and "Red Pepper")

6. Rocking

7. Round And Round In A Swing

8. Jump The River

9. Climbing

10. Ping Pong

11. Sitting Up and Lying Down

12. Fit As A Fiddle and Ready To Go

Fit as a fid - dle, Ex - er-cise my fin - gers ev -'ry day;

Fit as a fid - dle, Ex - er-cise will make my fin - gers play.

Group IV

1. Deep Breathing

2. Walking On A Sunny, Then A Cloudy Day

3. Skipping On A Sunny, Then A Cloudy Day

4. Cartwheels On A Sunny, Then A Cloudy Day

5. Jumping On A Sunny, Then A Cloudy Day

6. Running On A Sunny, Then A Cloudy Day

7. Walking Pigeon-toed

8. Wiggling Toes

9. See-Saw

10. Peeping Between Knees

11. Bouncing A Ball

12. Fit As A Fiddle and Ready To Go

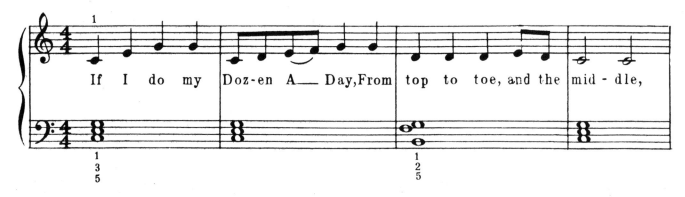

If I do my Doz-en A__ Day, From top to toe, and the mid - dle,

Then I know I'll al - ways__ stay, Just as fit as a fid - dle.

Group V

1. Walking Up A Hill

2. Taking Deep Breaths
While Walking Up A Hill

3. Running Up A Hill

4. Skipping Up A Hill

5. Cartwheels Up A Hill

6. Jumping Up A Hill

7. Boxing

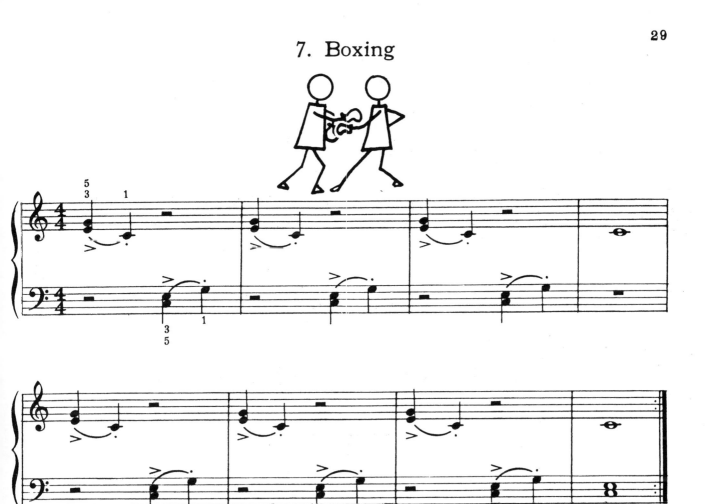

8. Spinning A Big Top

9. Rolling A Hoop

10. Raising Arms Up and Up On Toes

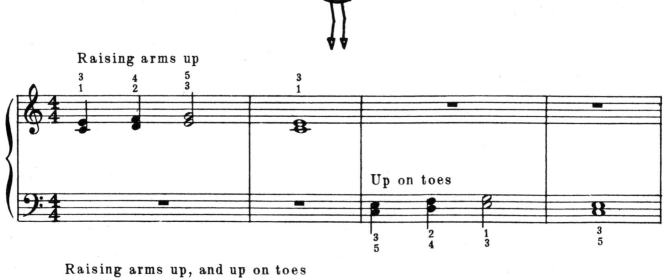

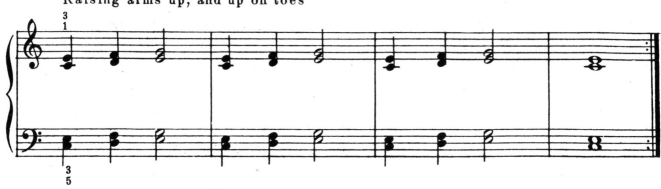

11. Riding Piggyback

12. Fit As A Fiddle and Ready To Go

A Doz-en A Day, be-fore I play, Keeps the kinks a-way; A

Doz-en A Day, Hip, Hip, Hoo-ray, Makes me feel O. K.